MACAROONS

BÉRENGÈRE ABRAHAM

PHOTOGRAPHS BY MARIE-JOSÉ JARRY

spruce

CONTENTS

TWICE AS TEMPTING

INTRODUCTION

Delicate and infinitely varied, macaroons are definitely the stars of the tea room! They can be made in a multitude of colors and flavors and, contrary to popular belief, macaroons are easy to make. With a little care and attention you too can make your favorites at home.

To achieve the perfect macaroon, it is essential that you follow some simple rules. The first rule is to separate the eggs the day before you use them, setting the whites aside in the refrigerator. "Ageing" the egg whites helps the macaroon shells to hold their shape and form a stronger crust; it also prevents them from sticking. Be sure to take the whites out of the refrigerator in good time to bring to room temperature before use. The second rule is to be careful about the "shell drying" time necessary to ensure that the macaroons form a crust and rise properly during cooking. Be patient and let the shells stand for a good hour at room temperature before putting them in the oven.

There are no rules when it comes to coloring the macaroons. Don't worry about over-coloring the shell mixture; the color will lose its intensity during cooking. You can find powdered or liquid food colorings in the baking section of supermarkets or specialist shops; you can also buy them online. They are both used in the same way although the powders are much more concentrated—a tiny pinch is enough.

Finally, macaroons will keep for several days in the refrigerator. Store them in layers separated by waxed paper in an airtight container. They are even better the day after they are made.

FOOLPROOF MACAROONS

Finely grind the ground almonds and confectioners' sugar in a blender.

Strain the mixture over a baking sheet and cook at 300°F (150°C) for 5–7 minutes. Let cool.

In a mixing bowl, beat the egg whites into snowy peaks using an electric hand mixer. When they start to stiffen, gradually add the superfine sugar, beating constantly.

Add a few drops of food coloring.

Continue beating the mixture until smooth.

Strain the almond-sugar mixture over the egg whites and fold in, using a silicone spatula.

Fill a pastry bag with this mixture and pipe out 30 x 1½-inch (4.5-cm) uniform circles onto a baking sheet lined with baking parchment

Let the shells stand for at least 1 hour in a dry place until a crust forms on the surface, then cook for 10–12 minutes.

Let the shells cool, then pour a trickle of water between the parchment and the baking sheet.

Remove the shells using a small frosting spatula.

Spread a ganache over half the shells.

Top each shell with another shell to make the macaroons. Chill before serving.

NANCY MACAROON

There are many different kinds of macaroons; amaretti, for instance, are the best-known type of Italian macaroon. In France, the macaroons from Amiens are famous, as are those from Saint-Jean-de-Luz or Saint-Émilion. This recipe is for the town of Nancy's celebrated macaroons.

PREPARATION TIME 20 minutes
SHELL DRYING TIME 30 minutes
COOKING TIME 20–25 minutes

FOR THE SHELLS

Scant ¾ cup (100 g)
  confectioners' sugar
1 sachet vanilla sugar (around
  ½ tablespoon/7 g)
Generous ¾ cup (100 g)
  ground almonds
A few drops of bitter almond
  extract (optional)
2 large eggs

MAKES 20 MACAROONS

TO START Preheat the oven to 300°F (150°C).

TO MAKE THE SHELLS Mix together the confectioners' sugar, vanilla sugar, ground almonds, and if desired a few drops of bitter almond extract (for a stronger almond flavor). Separate the eggs and whisk the egg whites with a fork, then add them to the almond-sugar mixture. Use a silicone spatula to mix it all together into a smooth paste.

Fill a pastry bag with this mixture and pipe 20 x 1½-inch (4.5-cm) uniform circles onto a baking sheet lined with baking parchment. Lightly brush the top of each macaroon with water, then let them stand for 30 minutes.

Bake the macaroons for 20–25 minutes. Let the shells cool, then pour a trickle of water between the parchment and the baking sheet and remove the shells using a small frosting spatula.

CHOCOLATE MACAROON

If making this for chocoholics, make the ganache using chocolate with a high cocoa content. For a less pronounced taste, choose milk or hazelnut chocolate.

PREPARATION TIME 30 minutes
CHILLING TIME 12–24 hours
 + 1 hour
SHELL DRYING TIME 1 hour
COOKING TIME about 20 minutes

FOR THE SHELLS

2 large eggs
½ cup (60 g) ground almonds
¾ cup (110 g) confectioners' sugar
1½ tablespoons (20 g)
   superfine sugar
3 heaping tablespoons (25 g)
   unsweetened cocoa powder

FOR THE CHOCOLATE GANACHE

6 oz (175 g) dark chocolate
1¼ cups (300 ml) whipping cream

MAKES 15 MACAROONS

PREPARE AHEAD Separate the eggs and set the whites aside in the refrigerator for up to 24 hours. Bring to room temperature before making the macaroon shells the following day.

TO MAKE THE CHOCOLATE GANACHE Break the chocolate into small pieces and melt gently in a bowl set over a pan of barely simmering water, then pour in the cream and blend the mixture well, using a spatula. Remove from the heat and let cool. Chill in the refrigerator.

TO MAKE THE SHELLS Preheat the oven to 300°F (150°C). Finely grind the ground almonds and confectioners' sugar in a blender. Strain the mixture over a baking sheet and cook for 5–7 minutes. Let cool.

In a mixing bowl, beat the egg whites into snowy peaks using an electric hand mixer. When they start to stiffen, gradually add the superfine sugar, beating constantly. Add the cocoa powder and combine until evenly dispersed. Strain the almond-sugar mixture over the egg whites and fold in using a silicone spatula.

Fill a pastry bag with this mixture and pipe out 30 x 1½-inch (4.5-cm) uniform circles onto a baking sheet lined with baking parchment. Let stand for at least 1 hour in a dry place until a crust forms on the surface, then cook for 10–12 minutes. Let the shells cool, then pour a trickle of water between the parchment and the baking sheet and remove the shells using a small frosting spatula.

TO ASSEMBLE THE MACAROONS Spread the chocolate ganache over half the shells, then top them with the remaining shells. Chill for 1 hour before serving.

CARAMEL MACAROON WITH SALTED BUTTER

This delicious macaroon has a Breton touch! Use *beurre de baratte* or butter containing salt crystals, if you can, for truly authentic macaroons.

PREPARATION TIME 30 minutes
CHILLING TIME 12–24 hours
 + 2 hours + 1 hour
SHELL DRYING TIME 1 hour
COOKING TIME about 20 minutes

FOR THE SHELLS

2 large eggs
½ cup (60 g) ground almonds
¾ cup (110 g) confectioners' sugar
1½ tablespoons (20 g)
  superfine sugar
Brown food coloring

FOR THE SALTED BUTTER CARAMEL

3 heaping tablespoons (50 ml)
  whipping cream
4 tablespoons (60 g) superfine sugar
1 tablespoonful (15 g) softened
  beurre de baratte or semi-salted
  butter, cut into small pieces

MAKES 15 MACAROONS

PREPARE AHEAD Separate the eggs and set the whites aside in the refrigerator for up to 24 hours. Bring to room temperature before making the macaroon shells the following day.

TO MAKE THE CARAMEL Pour the cream into a saucepan and heat gently over a low heat. In another saucepan heat the superfine sugar with 1 tablespoonful of water until it colors and forms a golden caramel. Remove from the heat and add the lukewarm cream to the caramel, along with the butter. Blend the mixture well and let cool. Chill in the refrigerator for at least 2 hours.

TO MAKE THE SHELLS Preheat the oven to 300°F (150°C). Finely grind the ground almonds and confectioners' sugar in a blender. Strain the mixture over a baking sheet and cook for 5–7 minutes. Let cool.

In a mixing bowl, beat the egg whites into snowy peaks using an electric hand mixer. When they start to stiffen, gradually add the superfine sugar, beating constantly. Add a few drops of brown coloring and combine until the coloring is evenly dispersed. Strain the almond-sugar mixture over the egg whites and fold in using a silicone spatula.

Fill a pastry bag with this mixture and pipe out 30 x 1½-inch (4.5-cm) uniform circles onto a baking sheet lined with baking parchment. Let stand for at least 1 hour in a dry place until a crust forms on the surface, then cook for 10–12 minutes. Let the shells cool, then pour a trickle of water between the parchment and the baking sheet and remove the shells using a small frosting spatula.

TO ASSEMBLE THE MACAROONS Spread the salted butter caramel over half the shells, then top them with the remaining shells. Chill for 1 hour before serving.

COFFEE MACAROON

This unbeatable recipe is the perfect accompaniment
to an espresso or cappuccino.

PREPARATION TIME 30 minutes
CHILLING TIME 12–24 hours
  + 1 hour
SHELL DRYING TIME 1 hour
COOKING TIME about 30 minutes

FOR THE SHELLS

2 large eggs
½ cup (60 g) ground almonds
¾ cup (110 g) confectioners' sugar
1½ tablespoons (20 g)
  superfine sugar
A few drops of coffee essence

FOR THE COFFEE GANACHE

2 eggs
Scant ⅔ cup (135 g) superfine sugar
6½ oz (1⅝ sticks/180 g)
  softened butter
1 heaping tablespoon freeze-dried
  coffee powder

MAKES 15 MACAROONS

PREPARE AHEAD Separate the eggs and set the whites aside in the refrigerator for up to 24 hours. Bring to room temperature before making the macaroon shells the following day.

TO MAKE THE COFFEE GANACHE Break the eggs into a bowl and beat with a fork. In a saucepan, mix the superfine sugar with 3 tablespoons of water and heat to 250°F (120°C), using a candy thermometer to check the temperature. Pour this syrup over the eggs and mix well. Chill in the refrigerator.

THE FOLLOWING DAY Add the softened butter and freeze-dried coffee powder to the syrup and beat until smooth with an electric beater. Set aside.

TO MAKE THE SHELLS Preheat the oven to 300°F (150°C). Finely grind the ground almonds and confectioners' sugar in a blender. Strain the mixture over a baking sheet and cook for 5–7 minutes. Let cool.

In a mixing bowl, beat the egg whites into snowy peaks using an electric hand mixer. When they start to stiffen, gradually add the superfine sugar, beating constantly. Add the coffee essence and combine until evenly dispersed. Strain the almond-sugar mixture over the egg whites and fold in using a silicone spatula.

Fill a pastry bag with this mixture and pipe out 30 x 1½-inch (4.5-cm) uniform circles onto a baking sheet lined with baking parchment. Let stand for at least 1 hour in a dry place until a crust forms on the surface, then cook for 10–12 minutes. Let the shells cool, then pour a trickle of water between the parchment and the baking sheet and remove the shells using a small frosting spatula.

TO ASSEMBLE THE MACAROONS Spread the coffee ganache over half the shells, then top them with the remaining shells. Chill for 1 hour before serving.

PRALINE MACAROON

A praline is a mixture of crushed almonds, hazelnuts, and confectioners' sugar. Make these macaroons even prettier by sprinkling them with praline just before serving.

PREPARATION TIME 30 minutes
CHILLING TIME 12–24 hours
  + 1 hour
SHELL DRYING TIME 1 hour
COOKING TIME about 20 minutes

FOR THE SHELLS

2 large eggs
½ cup (60 g) ground almonds
¾ cup (110 g) confectioners' sugar
1½ tablespoons (20 g)
  superfine sugar
Brown food coloring

FOR THE PRALINE CREAM

1 egg
2 tablespoons (30 g) superfine sugar
3 heaping tablespoons (25 g)
  plain flour
2 tablespoons (30 g)
  powdered praline
½ cup (120 ml) milk
2 heaping tablespoons (30 g)
  softened butter, cut into
  small pieces

MAKES 15 MACAROONS

PREPARE AHEAD Separate the eggs and set the whites aside in the refrigerator for up to 24 hours. Bring to room temperature before making the macaroon shells the following day.

TO MAKE THE PRALINE CREAM Break the egg into a bowl with the superfine sugar and beat with a fork. Add the flour and powdered praline and mix well. Gradually add the milk, then pour the mixture into a saucepan and heat gently until lukewarm. Add the butter and cook gently until the mixture thickens, stirring constantly. Remove from the heat and let cool. Chill in the refrigerator.

TO MAKE THE SHELLS Preheat the oven to 300°F (150°C). Finely grind the ground almonds and confectioners' sugar in a blender. Strain the mixture over a baking sheet and cook for 5–7 minutes. Let cool.

In a mixing bowl, beat the egg whites into snowy peaks, using an electric hand mixer. When they start to stiffen, gradually add the superfine sugar, beating constantly. Add a few drops of brown food coloring and combine until evenly dispersed. Strain the almond-sugar mixture over the egg whites and fold in using a silicone spatula.

Fill a pastry bag with this mixture and pipe out 30 x 1½-inch (4.5-cm) uniform circles onto a baking sheet lined with baking parchment. Let stand for at least 1 hour in a dry place until a crust forms on the surface, then cook for 10–12 minutes. Let the shells cool, then pour a trickle of water between the parchment and the baking sheet and remove the shells using a small frosting spatula.

TO ASSEMBLE THE MACAROONS Spread the praline cream over half the shells, then top them with the remaining shells. Chill for 1 hour before serving.

PISTACHIO MACAROON

With its mild flavor and green color, the pistachio nut holds many surprises and adds a delicate note to this recipe.

PREPARATION TIME 30 minutes
CHILLING TIME 12–24 hours
  + 1 hour
SHELL DRYING TIME 1 hour
COOKING TIME about 25 minutes

FOR THE SHELLS

2 large eggs
½ cup (60 g) ground almonds
¾ cup (110 g) confectioners' sugar
1½ tablespoons (20 g)
  superfine sugar
Green food coloring

FOR THE PISTACHIO GANACHE

Scant ½ cup (100 ml)
  whipping cream
½ cup (50 g) pistachio paste
2 sachets vanilla sugar (around
  1 tablespoon/14 g)
2 egg yolks
1½ tablespoons (20 g)
  softened butter

MAKES 15 MACAROONS

PREPARE AHEAD Separate the eggs and set the whites aside in the refrigerator for up to 24 hours. Bring to room temperature before making the macaroon shells the following day. Reserve the yolks to use in the ganache.

TO MAKE THE PISTACHIO GANACHE Gently heat the whipping cream in a saucepan and dissolve the pistachio paste in it. Add 1 sachet of the vanilla sugar and bring to a boil. In a mixing bowl, blend together the egg yolks and the second sachet of vanilla sugar and add to the cream-pistachio mixture. Heat to 200°F (95°C), using a candy thermometer to check the temperature. Let cool, then add the softened butter, mix in well, and chill in the refrigerator.

TO MAKE THE SHELLS Preheat the oven to 300°F (150°C). Finely grind the ground almonds and confectioners' sugar in a blender. Strain the mixture over a baking sheet and cook for 5–7 minutes. Let cool.

In a mixing bowl, beat the egg whites into snowy peaks using an electric hand mixer. When they start to stiffen, gradually add the superfine sugar, beating constantly. Add a few drops of green food coloring and combine until evenly dispersed. Strain the almond-sugar mixture over the egg whites and fold in using a silicone spatula.

Fill a pastry bag with this mixture and pipe out 30 x 1½-inch (4.5-cm) uniform circles onto a baking sheet lined with baking parchment. Let stand for at least 1 hour in a dry place until a crust forms on the surface, then cook for 10–12 minutes. Let the shells cool, then pour a trickle of water between the parchment and the baking sheet and remove the shells using a small frosting spatula.

TO ASSEMBLE THE MACAROONS Spread the pistachio cream over half the shells, then top them with the remaining shells. Chill for 1 hour before serving.

LICORICE MACAROON

Don't be misled by its dark and somber appearance; this macaroon is deliciously sweet and creamy.

PREPARATION TIME 30 minutes
CHILLING TIME 12–24 hours
  + 1 hour
SHELL DRYING TIME 1 hour
COOKING TIME about 20 minutes

FOR THE SHELLS

2 large eggs
½ cup (60 g) ground almonds
¾ cup (110 g) confectioners' sugar
1½ tablespoons (20 g)
  superfine sugar
Black food coloring

FOR THE LICORICE GANACHE

⅔ cup (150 ml) whipping cream
2 pieces of licorice or 4–5 pastilles
1 teaspoon clear honey
2¾ oz (75 g) white chocolate

MAKES 15 MACAROONS

PREPARE AHEAD Separate the eggs and set the whites aside in the refrigerator for up to 24 hours. Bring to room temperature before making the macaroon shells the following day.

TO MAKE THE LICORICE GANACHE Gently heat 3 heaping tablespoons (50 ml) of the whipping cream in a saucepan and dissolve the licorice in it. When the mixture is quite smooth, add the honey, then set aside. Break the chocolate into small pieces and melt gently in a bowl set over a pan of barely simmering water. Pour in the licorice cream and blend well. Remove from the heat and add the remaining cream. Chill in the refrigerator.

TO MAKE THE SHELLS Preheat the oven to 300°F (150°C). Finely grind the ground almonds and confectioners' sugar in a blender. Strain the mixture over a baking sheet and cook for 5–7 minutes. Let cool.

In a mixing bowl, beat the egg whites into snowy peaks using an electric hand mixer. When they start to stiffen, gradually add the superfine sugar, beating constantly. Add a few drops of black food coloring and combine until evenly dispersed. Strain the almond-sugar mixture over the egg whites and fold in using a silicone spatula.

Fill a pastry bag with this mixture and pipe out 30 x 1½-inch (4.5-cm) uniform circles onto a baking sheet lined with baking parchment. Let stand for at least 1 hour in a dry place until a crust forms on the surface, then cook for 10–12 minutes. Let the shells cool, then pour a trickle of water between the parchment and the baking sheet and remove the shells using a small frosting spatula.

TO ASSEMBLE THE MACAROONS Spread the licorice ganache over half the shells, then top them with the remaining shells. Chill for 1 hour before serving.

ROSE MACAROON

Here's a very feminine recipe for evenings with girlfriends.
Serve with a glass of champagne, of course!

PREPARATION TIME 30 minutes
CHILLING TIME 12–24 hours
   + 1 hour
SHELL DRYING TIME 1 hour
COOKING TIME about 25 minutes

FOR THE SHELLS

2 large eggs
½ cup (60 g) ground almonds
¾ cup (110 g) confectioners' sugar
1½ tablespoons (20 g)
   superfine sugar
Pink food coloring

FOR THE ROSE GANACHE

⅔ cup (150 ml) whipping cream
2 tablespoons rose water
2¾ oz (75 g) white chocolate

MAKES 15 MACAROONS

PREPARE AHEAD Separate the eggs and set the whites aside in the refrigerator for up to 24 hours. Bring to room temperature before making the macaroon shells the following day.

TO MAKE THE ROSE GANACHE Put 3 heaping tablespoons (50 ml) of the whipping cream in a saucepan, add the rose water, and heat gently. When the mixture comes to simmering point, remove from the heat and set aside. Break the chocolate into small pieces and melt gently in a bowl set over a pan of barely simmering water, then add the rose cream. Blend well, remove from the heat, and add the remaining cream. Chill in the refrigerator.

TO MAKE THE SHELLS Preheat the oven to 300°F (150°C). Finely grind the ground almonds and confectioners' sugar in a blender. Strain the mixture over a baking sheet and cook for 5–7 minutes. Let cool.

In a mixing bowl, beat the egg whites into snowy peaks using an electric hand mixer. When they start to stiffen, gradually add the superfine sugar, beating constantly. Add a few drops of pink food coloring and combine until evenly dispersed. Strain the almond-sugar mixture over the egg whites and fold in using a silicone spatula.

Fill a pastry bag with this mixture and pipe out 30 x 1½-inch (4.5-cm) uniform circles onto a baking sheet lined with baking parchment. Let stand for at least 1 hour in a dry place until a crust forms on the surface, then cook for 10–12 minutes. Let the shells cool, then pour a trickle of water between the parchment and the baking sheet and remove the shells using a small frosting spatula.

TO ASSEMBLE THE MACAROONS Lightly whip the rose ganache using an electric mixer. Spread it over half the shells, then top them with the remaining shells. Chill for 1 hour before serving.

LEMON MACAROON

This tangy, prettily colored lemon macaroon is filled
with lemon curd. For a surefire success, serve it with
a smoked tea such as lapsang souchong.

PREPARATION TIME 30 minutes
CHILLING TIME 12–24 hours
  + 1 hour
SHELL DRYING TIME 1 hour
COOKING TIME about 25 minutes

FOR THE SHELLS

2 large eggs
½ cup (60 g) ground almonds
¾ cup (110 g) confectioners' sugar
1½ tablespoons (20 g)
  superfine sugar
Yellow food coloring
1 tablespoon lemon juice

FOR THE LEMON CURD

2 eggs
4 tablespoons (50 g) turbinado sugar
1 teaspoon cornstarch
Juice of 2 lemons

MAKES 15 MACAROONS

PREPARE AHEAD Separate the eggs and set the whites aside in the refrigerator
for up to 24 hours. Bring to room temperature before making the macaroon shells
the following day.

TO MAKE THE LEMON CURD Put the eggs, turbinado sugar, and cornstarch
in a mixing bowl and beat well. Add the lemon juice, then pour the mixture into
a saucepan. Cook over a gentle heat for 5–7 minutes, beating continually until the
mixture thickens. Let the lemon curd cool, then chill in the refrigerator.

TO MAKE THE SHELLS Preheat the oven to 300°F (150°C). Finely grind
the ground almonds and confectioners' sugar in a blender. Strain the mixture over
a baking sheet and cook for 5–7 minutes. Let cool.
   In a mixing bowl, beat the egg whites into snowy peaks using an electric
hand mixer. When they start to stiffen, gradually add the superfine sugar, beating
constantly. Add a few drops of yellow food coloring and the lemon juice and
combine until evenly dispersed. Strain the almond-sugar mixture over the
egg whites and fold in using a silicone spatula.
   Fill a pastry bag with this mixture and pipe out 30 x 1½-inch (4.5-cm) uniform
circles onto a baking sheet lined with baking parchment. Let stand for at least 1 hour
in a dry place until a crust forms on the surface, then cook for 10–12 minutes. Let
the shells cool, then pour a trickle of water between the parchment and the baking
sheet and remove the shells using a small frosting spatula.

TO ASSEMBLE THE MACAROONS Spread the lemon curd over half the
shells, then top them with the remaining shells. Chill for 1 hour before serving.

CHERRY MACAROON

This spring-fresh macaroon can be made in any season with frozen cherries. Use sweet, sour (Morello), or black cherries.

PREPARATION TIME 30 minutes
CHILLING TIME 12–24 hours
    + 1 hour
SHELL DRYING TIME 1 hour
COOKING TIME about 30 minutes

FOR THE SHELLS

2 large eggs
½ cup (60 g) ground almonds
¾ cup (110 g) confectioners' sugar
1½ tablespoons (20 g)
    superfine sugar
Red and brown food coloring

FOR THE CHERRY CONFITURE

1 vanilla bean
10½ oz (300 g) pitted cherries,
    fresh or frozen
6 tablespoons (75 g) superfine sugar
1 tablespoon (15 g) pectin or other
    gelling agent for jams

MAKES 15 MACAROONS

PREPARE AHEAD Separate the eggs and set the whites aside in the refrigerator for up to 24 hours. Bring to room temperature before making the macaroon shells the following day.

TO MAKE THE CHERRY CONFITURE Using a small knife, split the vanilla bean in half lengthwise, then scrape out the seeds. Put the cherries in a saucepan with 1 tablespoon of water, add the sugar and vanilla seeds, then cook on a low heat for 7–10 minutes. (If using frozen cherries, do not add water and cook for 5 minutes longer.) Pour the mixture into a blender and blend well, then pour this purée back into the saucepan, add the pectin, and heat gently for 5 minutes. Set aside.

TO MAKE THE SHELLS Preheat the oven to 300°F (150°C). Finely grind the ground almonds and confectioners' sugar in a blender. Strain the mixture over a baking sheet and cook for 5–7 minutes. Let cool.

In a mixing bowl, beat the egg whites into snowy peaks using an electric hand mixer. When they start to stiffen, gradually add the superfine sugar, beating constantly. Add a few drops each of red and brown food coloring and combine until evenly dispersed. Strain the almond-sugar mixture over the egg whites and fold in using a silicone spatula.

Fill a pastry bag with this mixture and pipe out 30 x 1½-inch (4.5-cm) uniform circles onto a baking sheet lined with baking parchment. Let stand for at least 1 hour in a dry place until a crust forms on the surface, then cook for 10–12 minutes. Let the shells cool, then pour a trickle of water between the parchment and the baking sheet and remove the shells using a small frosting spatula.

TO ASSEMBLE THE MACAROONS Spread the cherry confiture over half the shells, then top them with the remaining shells. Chill for 1 hour before serving.

BLUEBERRY MACAROON

These sweet and slightly sugary little berries give this macaroon a delicious flavor. Fill your basket with blueberries during a trip to the mountains and make this very special cookie.

PREPARATION TIME 30 minutes
CHILLING TIME 12–24 hours
  + 1 hour
SHELL DRYING TIME 1 hour
COOKING TIME about 20 minutes

FOR THE SHELLS

2 large eggs
½ cup (60 g) ground almonds
¾ cup (110 g) confectioners' sugar
1½ tablespoons (20 g)
   superfine sugar
Violet food coloring

FOR THE BLUEBERRY GANACHE

1 cup (100 g) fresh blueberries
5½ oz (150 g) white chocolate
3 heaping tablespoons (50 ml)
   whipping cream

MAKES 15 MACAROONS

PREPARE AHEAD Separate the eggs and set the whites aside in the refrigerator for up to 24 hours. Bring to room temperature before making the macaroon shells the following day.

TO MAKE THE BLUEBERRY GANACHE Process the fruit in a blender, then strain through a fine sieve. Break the chocolate into small pieces and melt gently in a bowl set over a pan of barely simmering water, then pour in the cream. Remove from the heat and add the blueberry juice. Use a spatula to blend well, then chill in the refrigerator.

TO MAKE THE SHELLS Preheat the oven to 300°F (150°C). Finely grind the ground almonds and confectioners' sugar in a blender. Strain the mixture over an oven tray and cook for 5–7 minutes. Let cool.

In a mixing bowl, beat the egg whites into snowy peaks using an electric hand-mixer. When they start to stiffen, gradually add the superfine sugar, beating constantly. Add a few drops of violet food coloring and combine until evenly dispersed. Strain the almond-sugar mixture over the egg whites and fold in using a silicone spatula.

Fill a pastry bag with this mixture and pipe out 30 x 1½-inch (4.5-cm) uniform circles onto a baking sheet lined with baking parchment. Let stand for at least 1 hour in a dry place until a crust forms on the surface, then cook for 10–12 minutes. Let the shells cool, then pour a trickle of water between the parchment and the baking sheet and remove the shells using a small frosting spatula.

TO ASSEMBLE THE MACAROONS Spread the blueberry ganache over half the shells, then top them with the remaining shells. If the ganache is too solid when removed from the refrigerator, break it up with a small spatula. Chill for 1 hour before serving.

RASPBERRY MACAROON

This recipe is a smash hit: a macaroon filled with a delicious raspberry confiture. If desired, remove the seeds by straining the raspberry juice through a very fine conical sieve.

PREPARATION TIME 30 minutes
CHILLING TIME 12–24 hours
    + 1 hour
SHELL DRYING TIME 1 hour
COOKING TIME about 30 minutes

FOR THE SHELLS

2 large eggs
½ cup (60 g) ground almonds
¾ cup (110 g) confectioners' sugar
1½ tablespoons (20 g)
    superfine sugar
Red food coloring

FOR THE RASPBERRY CONFITURE

1 cup (125 g) raspberries
6 tablespoons (75 g) superfine sugar
1 teaspoon (5 g) pectin or other
    gelling agent for jams
Juice of ½ lemon

MAKES 15 MACAROONS

PREPARE AHEAD Separate the eggs and set the whites aside in the refrigerator for up to 24 hours. Bring to room temperature before making the macaroon shells the following day.

TO MAKE THE RASPBERRY CONFITURE Process the fruit in a blender with 1 tablespoon of water and pour this purée into a saucepan. Add the superfine sugar and the pectin. Bring gently to boiling point and simmer for 5 minutes, then add the lemon juice. Blend in well and cook for 5 minutes more. Let cool and set aside.

TO MAKE THE SHELLS Preheat the oven to 300°F (150°C). Finely grind the ground almonds and confectioners' sugar in a blender. Strain the mixture over a baking sheet and cook for 5–7 minutes. Let cool.

In a mixing bowl, beat the egg whites into snowy peaks, using an electric hand mixer. When they start to stiffen, gradually add the superfine sugar, beating constantly. Add a few drops of red food coloring and combine until evenly dispersed. Strain the almond-sugar mixture over the egg whites and fold in using a silicone spatula.

Fill a pastry bag with this mixture and pipe out 30 x 1½-inch (4.5-cm) uniform circles onto a baking sheet lined with baking parchment. Let stand for at least 1 hour in a dry place until a crust forms on the surface, then cook for 10–12 minutes. Let the shells cool, then pour a trickle of water between the parchment and the baking sheet and remove the shells using a small frosting spatula.

TO ASSEMBLE THE MACAROONS Spread the raspberry confiture over half the shells, then top them with the remaining shells. Chill for 1 hour before serving.

PASSION FRUIT MACAROON

You will be delighted with this exotic recipe. The tangy taste of passion fruit goes wonderfully with the crunch of the macaroons. If you cannot find passion fruit or are in a hurry, replace the fruit pulp with ½ cup (120 ml) passion fruit juice and halve the quantity of sugar.

PREPARATION TIME 30 minutes
CHILLING TIME 12–24 hours
  + 1 hour
SHELL DRYING TIME 1 hour
COOKING TIME about 30 minutes

FOR THE SHELLS

2 large eggs
½ cup (60 g) ground almonds
¾ cup (110 g) confectioners' sugar
1½ tablespoons (20 g)
  superfine sugar
Yellow and orange food coloring

FOR THE PASSION FRUIT GANACHE

8 passion fruit
Scant 4 tablespoons (50 g)
  superfine sugar
Juice of ½ lemon
2 teaspoons (10 g) pectin or other
  gelling agent for jams

MAKES 15 MACAROONS

PREPARE AHEAD Separate the eggs and set the whites aside in the refrigerator for up to 24 hours. Bring to room temperature before making the macaroon shells the following day.

TO MAKE THE PASSION FRUIT GANACHE Cut the passion fruit in half and scrape out the pulp. Put it in a saucepan with half the superfine sugar and the lemon juice, then cook gently over a low heat for 5 minutes. Strain the mixture through a fine-mesh conical sieve to obtain a smooth juice. Add the remaining sugar and the pectin, then bring to a boil and cook for 5 minutes more. Set aside.

TO MAKE THE SHELLS Preheat the oven to 300°F (150°C). Finely grind the ground almonds and confectioners' sugar in a blender. Strain the mixture over a baking sheet and cook for 5–7 minutes. Let cool.

In a mixing bowl, beat the egg whites into snowy peaks using an electric hand mixer. When they start to stiffen, gradually add the superfine sugar, beating constantly. Add a few drops of yellow food coloring and 1 drop of orange food coloring and combine until evenly dispersed. Strain the almond-sugar mixture over the egg whites and fold in, using a silicone spatula.

Fill a pastry bag with this mixture and pipe out 30 x 1½-inch (4.5-cm) uniform circles onto a baking sheet lined with baking parchment. Let stand for at least 1 hour in a dry place until a crust forms on the surface, then cook for 10–12 minutes. Let the shells cool, then pour a trickle of water between the parchment and the baking sheet and remove the shells using a small frosting spatula.

TO ASSEMBLE THE MACAROONS Spread the passion fruit ganache over half the shells, then top them with the remaining shells. Chill for 1 hour before serving.

MILK CHOCOLATE AND VANILLA MACAROON

Notes of almond, vanilla, and caramel give a delicious flavor to this macaroon. This is a recipe certain to please all foodies.

PREPARATION TIME 30 minutes
CHILLING TIME 12–24 hours
  + 1 hour
SHELL DRYING TIME 1 hour
COOKING TIME about 20 minutes

FOR THE SHELLS

2 large eggs
½ cup (60 g) ground almonds
¾ cup (110 g) confectioners' sugar
1½ tablespoons (20 g)
  superfine sugar
2 tablespoons (15 g) unsweetened
  cocoa powder
½ vanilla bean

FOR THE MILK
CHOCOLATE GANACHE

2½ oz (60 g) milk chocolate
2 tablespoons (25 g) semi-salted
  butter, cut into small pieces
2 tablespoons whipping cream
½ vanilla bean

MAKES 15 MACAROONS

PREPARE AHEAD Separate the eggs and set the whites aside in the refrigerator for up to 24 hours. Bring to room temperature before making the macaroon shells the following day.

TO MAKE THE MILK CHOCOLATE GANACHE Break the chocolate into small pieces and melt gently in a bowl set over a pan of barely simmering water. Add the butter and pour in the cream. Using a small knife, split the half vanilla bean in half lengthwise and scrape out the seeds. Add them to the mixture and blend in well, using a silicone spatula. Remove from the heat and let cool. Chill in the refrigerator.

TO MAKE THE SHELLS Preheat the oven to 300°F (150°C). Finely grind the ground almonds and confectioners' sugar in a blender. Strain the mixture over a baking sheet and cook for 5–7 minutes. Let cool.

In a mixing bowl, beat the egg whites into snowy peaks using an electric hand mixer. When they start to stiffen, gradually add the superfine sugar, beating constantly. Add the cocoa powder and combine until evenly dispersed. Strain the almond-sugar mix over the egg whites and fold in using a silicone spatula. Split the half vanilla bean in half lengthways and scrape out the seeds, then add them to the mixture and blend in well.

Fill a pastry bag with this mixture and pipe out 30 x 1½-inch (4.5-cm) uniform circles onto a baking sheet lined with baking parchment. Let stand for at least 1 hour in a dry place until a crust forms on the surface, then cook for 10–12 minutes. Let the shells cool, then pour a trickle of water between the parchment and the baking sheet and remove the shells using a small frosting spatula.

TO ASSEMBLE THE MACAROONS Spread the milk chocolate ganache over half the shells, then top them with the remaining shells. Chill for 1 hour before serving.

VIOLET AND WHITE CHOCOLATE MACAROON

Flowery and delicate, this is definitely a feminine macaroon!
For a more or less intense result, add violet essence to taste.

PREPARATION TIME 30 minutes
CHILLING TIME 12–24 hours
    + 1 hour
SHELL DRYING TIME 1 hour
COOKING TIME about 20 minutes

FOR THE SHELLS

2 large eggs
½ cup (60 g) ground almonds
¾ cup (110 g) confectioners' sugar
1½ tablespoons (20 g)
    superfine sugar
Violet food coloring

FOR THE WHITE
CHOCOLATE GANACHE

3½ oz (100 g) white chocolate
2 tablespoons whipping cream
1 teaspoon violet essence

MAKES 15 MACAROONS

PREPARE AHEAD Separate the eggs and set the whites aside in the refrigerator for up to 24 hours. Bring to room temperature before making the macaroon shells the following day.

TO MAKE THE WHITE CHOCOLATE GANACHE Break the chocolate into small pieces and melt gently with the whipping cream in a bowl set over a pan of barely simmering water. Remove from the heat, add the violet essence, and let cool. Chill in the refrigerator.

TO MAKE THE SHELLS Preheat the oven to 300°F (150°C). Finely grind the ground almonds and confectioners' sugar in a blender. Strain the mixture over a baking sheet and cook for 5–7 minutes. Let cool.

In a mixing bowl, beat the egg whites into snowy peaks using an electric hand mixer. When they start to stiffen, gradually add the superfine sugar, beating constantly. Add a few drops of violet food coloring and combine until evenly dispersed. Strain the almond-sugar mixture over the egg whites and fold in using a silicone spatula.

Fill a pastry bag with this mixture and pipe out 30 x 1½-inch (4.5-cm) uniform circles onto a baking sheet lined with baking parchment. Let stand for at least 1 hour in a dry place until a crust forms on the surface, then cook for 10–12 minutes. Let the shells cool, then pour a trickle of water between the parchment and the baking sheet and remove the shells using a small frosting spatula.

TO ASSEMBLE THE MACAROONS Spread the white chocolate ganache over half the shells, then top them with the remaining shells. Chill for 1 hour before serving.

GINGERSNAP AND VANILLA MACAROON

Only sprinkle over the crushed gingersnap cookies after the crust has formed on the unbaked macaroon shells, otherwise they will not rise properly.

PREPARATION TIME 30 minutes
CHILLING TIME 12–24 hours
  + 1 hour
SHELL DRYING TIME 1 hour
COOKING TIME about 25 minutes

FOR THE SHELLS

2 large eggs
½ cup (60 g) ground almonds
¾ cup (110 g) confectioners' sugar
1½ tablespoons (20 g)
  superfine sugar
5 gingersnap cookies, crushed

FOR THE VANILLA GANACHE

1 vanilla bean
⅔ cup (150 ml) whipping cream
1 teaspoon clear honey
2¾ oz (75 g) white chocolate

MAKES 15 MACAROONS

PREPARE AHEAD Separate the eggs and set the whites aside in the refrigerator for up to 24 hours. Bring to room temperature before making the macaroon shells the following day.

TO MAKE THE VANILLA GANACHE Using a small knife, split the vanilla bean in half lengthwise and scrape out the seeds. Add them to 3 heaping tablespoons (50 ml) of whipping cream and heat gently. When the mixture is lukewarm, stir in the honey and set aside. Break the chocolate into small pieces and melt gently in a bowl set over a pan of barely simmering water, then pour in the vanilla cream and blend the mixture well. Remove from the heat and add the remaining cream, then chill in the refrigerator until the following day.

TO MAKE THE SHELLS Preheat the oven to 300°F (150°C). Finely grind the ground almonds and confectioners' sugar in a blender. Strain the mixture over a baking sheet and cook for 5–7 minutes. Let cool.

In a mixing bowl, beat the egg whites into snowy peaks using an electric hand mixer. When they start to stiffen, gradually add the superfine sugar, beating constantly. Strain the almond-sugar mixture over the egg whites and fold in using a silicone spatula.

Fill a pastry bag with this mixture and pipe out 30 x 1½-inch (4.5-cm) uniform circles onto a baking sheet lined with baking parchment. Let stand for at least 1 hour in a dry place until a crust forms on the surface. Sprinkle the macaroon shells with the crushed gingersnap cookies, then cook for 10–12 minutes. Let the shells cool, then pour a trickle of water between the parchment and the baking sheet and remove the shells using a small frosting spatula.

TO ASSEMBLE THE MACAROONS Lightly beat the vanilla ganache and spread it over half the shells, then top them with the remaining shells. Chill for 1 hour before serving.

CHESTNUT AND HAZELNUT MACAROON

The sweet, creamy allure of this delicious macaroon makes it a seductive fall treat. If time is short, use ready-made chestnut cream.

PREPARATION TIME 30 minutes
CHILLING TIME 12–24 hours
+ 1 hour
SHELL DRYING TIME 1 hour
COOKING TIME 35–55 minutes

FOR THE SHELLS

2 large eggs
¼ cup (30 g) ground almonds
¼ cup (30 g) ground hazelnuts
¾ cup (110 g) confectioners' sugar
1½ tablespoons (20 g)
  superfine sugar
Brown food coloring

FOR THE CHESTNUT CREAM

1 vanilla bean
6 oz (200 g) chestnuts
  (canned or frozen)
1½ tablespoons (20 g)
  superfine sugar

MAKES 15 MACAROONS

PREPARE AHEAD Separate the eggs and set the whites aside in the refrigerator for up to 24 hours. Bring to room temperature before making the macaroon shells the following day.

TO MAKE THE CHESTNUT CREAM Using a small knife, split the vanilla bean in half lengthwise and scrape out the seeds. Put the vanilla bean and seeds in a saucepan with the chestnuts and cover with water. Bring to a boil, cover, and let simmer for 15 minutes. Let cool, then blend the mixture to a smooth purée. Set aside.

In a saucepan, mix the superfine sugar with a little water to make a thick syrup. Heat gently until it starts to bubble, then add the chestnut purée. Remove from the heat and let cool. Chill in the refrigerator.

TO MAKE THE SHELLS Preheat the oven to 300°F (150°C). Finely grind the ground almonds, ground hazelnuts, and confectioners' sugar in a blender. Strain the mixture over a baking sheet and cook for 5–7 minutes. Let cool.

In a mixing bowl, beat the egg whites into snowy peaks using an electric hand mixer. When they start to stiffen, gradually add the superfine sugar, beating constantly. Add a few drops of brown food coloring and combine until evenly dispersed. Strain the almond-sugar mixture over the egg whites and fold in using a silicone spatula.

Fill a pastry bag with this mixture and pipe out 30 x 1½-inch (4.5-cm) uniform circles onto a baking sheet lined with baking parchment. Let stand for at least 1 hour in a dry place until a crust forms on the surface, then cook for 10–12 minutes. Let the shells cool, then pour a trickle of water between the parchment and the baking sheet and remove the shells using a small frosting spatula.

TO ASSEMBLE THE MACAROONS Spread the chestnut cream over half the shells, then top them with the remaining shells. Chill for 1 hour before serving.

RHUBARB AND REDCURRANT MACAROON

You'll find that this macaroon is not at all sharp, while the combination of contrasting colors is very eye-catching. For a sweeter taste, add a teaspoonful of vanilla sugar to the confiture.

PREPARATION TIME 30 minutes
CHILLING TIME 12–24 hours
  + 1 hour
SHELL DRYING TIME 1 hour
COOKING TIME about 30 minutes

FOR THE SHELLS

2 large eggs
½ cup (60 g) ground almonds
¾ cup (110 g) confectioners' sugar
1½ tablespoons (20 g)
  superfine sugar
Green food coloring

FOR THE RHUBARB-REDCURRANT CONFITURE

1¼ cups (150 g) rhubarb, washed,
  peeled, and chopped
¾ cup (75 g) redcurrants,
  washed and trimmed
6 tablespoons (75 g) superfine sugar
2 teaspoons (10 g) pectin or other
  gelling agent for jams

MAKES 15 MACAROONS

PREPARE AHEAD Separate the eggs and set the whites aside in the refrigerator for up to 24 hours. Bring to room temperature before making the macaroon shells the following day.

TO MAKE THE RHUBARB-REDCURRANT CONFITURE Put the rhubarb and redcurrants in a saucepan, add 2 tablespoons of water and the superfine sugar, then cook for 10–15 minutes until the fruit is quite soft. Let cool slightly, then blend with a hand blender, add the pectin, and cook for 2–3 minutes more. Let cool, then chill in the refrigerator.

TO MAKE THE SHELLS Preheat the oven to 300°F (150°C). Finely grind the ground almonds and confectioners' sugar in a blender. Strain the mixture over a baking sheet and cook for 5–7 minutes. Let cool.

In a mixing bowl, beat the egg whites into snowy peaks using an electric hand mixer. When they start to stiffen, gradually add the superfine sugar, beating constantly. Add a few drops of green food coloring and combine until evenly dispersed. Strain the almond-sugar mixture over the egg whites and fold in using a silicone spatula.

Fill a pastry bag with this mixture and pipe out 30 x 1½-inch (4.5-cm) uniform circles onto a baking sheet lined with baking parchment. Let stand for at least 1 hour in a dry place until a crust forms on the surface, then cook for 10–12 minutes. Let the shells cool, then pour a trickle of water between the parchment and the baking sheet and remove the shells using a small frosting spatula.

TO ASSEMBLE THE MACAROONS Spread the confiture over half the shells, then top them with the remaining shells. Chill for 1 hour before serving.

NOUGATINE AND PEAR MACAROON

You may find crushed nougatine in the baking range at your supermarket. If not, try making your own by caramelizing flaked or ground almonds with superfine sugar in the oven, then crushing the mixture with a rolling pin.

PREPARATION TIME 30 minutes
CHILLING TIME 12–24 hours
  + 1 hour
SHELL DRYING TIME 1 hour
COOKING TIME 20–30 minutes

FOR THE SHELLS

2 large eggs
½ cup (60 g) ground almonds
¾ cup (110 g) confectioners' sugar
1½ tablespoons (20 g)
  superfine sugar
20 g crushed nougatine

FOR THE PEAR CONFITURE

3 small pears, peeled,
  cored, and diced
2¼ tablespoons (30 g)
  superfine sugar
1 tablespoon clear honey
2 teaspoons (10 g) pectin or other
  gelling agent for jams

MAKES 15 MACAROONS

PREPARE AHEAD Separate the eggs and set the whites aside in the refrigerator for up to 24 hours. Bring to room temperature before making the macaroon shells the following day.

TO MAKE THE PEAR CONFITURE Put the diced pears in a saucepan with the sugar, honey, and 2 tablespoons of water. Cook for 10 minutes, or until the fruit is quite soft. Let cool slightly, then blend with a hand blender, add the pectin, and cook for 2–3 minutes more. Let cool, then chill in the refrigerator.

TO MAKE THE SHELLS Preheat the oven to 300°F (150°C). Finely grind the ground almonds and confectioners' sugar in a blender. Strain the mixture over a baking sheet and cook for 5–7 minutes. Let cool.

In a mixing bowl, beat the egg whites into snowy peaks using an electric hand mixer. When they start to stiffen, gradually add the superfine sugar, beating constantly. Strain the almond-sugar mixture over the egg whites and fold in using a silicone spatula.

Fill a pastry bag with this mixture and pipe out 30 x 1½-inch (4.5-cm) uniform circles onto a baking sheet lined with baking parchment. Let stand for at least 1 hour in a dry place until a crust forms on the surface. Sprinkle them with the crushed nougatine and cook for 10–12 minutes. Let the shells cool, then pour a trickle of water between the parchment and the baking sheet and remove the shells using a small frosting spatula.

TO ASSEMBLE THE MACAROONS Spread the pear confiture over half the shells, then top them with the remaining shells. Chill for 1 hour before serving.

MANGO AND MASCARPONE MACAROON

In this recipe the ganache is made with mascarpone, like the base of a tiramisu, with a mango coulis added. The macaroons can be eaten, well-chilled, at any time of day.

PREPARATION TIME 45 minutes
CHILLING TIME 12–24 hours
  + 3 hours + 1 hour
SHELL DRYING TIME 1 hour
COOKING TIME about 20 minutes

FOR THE SHELLS

2 large eggs
½ cup (60 g) ground almonds
¾ cup (110 g) confectioners' sugar
1½ tablespoons (20 g)
  superfine sugar
Orange food coloring

FOR THE MANGO GANACHE

3 leaves gelatin
½ mango, well-ripened,
  peeled, and cubed
1 egg
4 scant tablespoons (50 g)
  superfine sugar
¼ cup (65 g) mascarpone
Pinch of salt

MAKES 15 MACAROONS

PREPARE AHEAD Separate the eggs and set the whites aside in the refrigerator for up to 24 hours. Bring to room temperature before making the macaroon shells the following day.

TO MAKE THE MANGO GANACHE Steep the gelatin in a bowl of cold water. Purée the mango cubes. Heat the purée gently, then remove from the heat, add the drained gelatin, and set aside. Separate the egg, then whisk the yolk in a bowl with the superfine sugar. Add the mascarpone and beat in well. In another bowl add the salt to the egg white and beat into snowy peaks using an electric hand mixer, then carefully fold it into the egg-mascarpone mixture. Pour in the mango purée and blend in well. Chill for at least 3 hours.

TO MAKE THE SHELLS Preheat the oven to 300°F (150°C). Finely grind the ground almonds and confectioners' sugar in a blender. Strain the mixture over a baking sheet and cook for 5–7 minutes. Let cool.

In a mixing bowl, beat the egg whites into snowy peaks using an electric hand mixer. When they start to stiffen, gradually add the superfine sugar, beating constantly. Add a few drops of orange food coloring and combine until evenly dispersed. Strain the almond-sugar mixture over the egg whites and fold in using a silicone spatula.

Fill a pastry bag with this mixture and pipe out 30 x 1½-inch (4.5-cm) uniform circles onto a baking sheet lined with baking parchment. Let stand for at least 1 hour in a dry place until a crust forms on the surface, then cook for 10–12 minutes. Let the shells cool, then pour a trickle of water between the parchment and the baking sheet and remove the shells using a small frosting spatula.

TO ASSEMBLE THE MACAROONS Spread the mango ganache over half the shells, then top them with the remaining shells. Chill for 1 hour before serving.

APPLE AND SPICE MACAROON

Be sure to brown the apples when making the confiture. This will give them a slightly caramelized taste that complements the spicy flavors of this delicious macaroon.

PREPARATION TIME 30 minutes
CHILLING TIME 12–24 hours
    + 1 hour
SHELL DRYING TIME 1 hour
COOKING TIME about 35 minutes

FOR THE SHELLS

2 large eggs
½ cup (60 g) ground almonds
¾ cup (110 g) confectioners' sugar
1½ tablespoons (20 g)
    superfine sugar
1 tablespoon (20 g) pumpkin pie
    spice (see below)

FOR THE PUMPKIN PIE SPICE BLEND

1 teaspoon (5 g) cinnamon
1 teaspoon (5 g) ground cloves
1 teaspoon (5 g) ground nutmeg
1 teaspoon (5 g) ground ginger

FOR THE APPLE CONFITURE

2 apples, peeled and cubed
4 tablespoons (50 g) turbinado sugar
Juice of ½ lemon
2 tablespoons (30 g) pectin or other
    gelling agent for jams

MAKES 15 MACAROONS

PREPARE AHEAD Separate the eggs and set the whites aside in the refrigerator for up to 24 hours. Bring to room temperature before making the macaroon shells the following day.

TO MAKE THE CONFITURE Put the apples in a saucepan along with the turbinado sugar, lemon juice, and 3 tablespoons water. Cook for 15 minutes until the mixture has softened. Continue cooking until the apples have caramelized, taking care that they do not burn. Add the pectin, cook for 2 minutes more, and let cool.

TO MAKE THE SHELLS Preheat the oven to 300°F (150°C). Finely grind the ground almonds and confectioners' sugar in a blender. Strain the mixture over a baking sheet and cook for 5–7 minutes. Let cool.

In a small dish, mix the spices to make the pumpkin pie spice blend. Set aside 1 teaspoon for sprinkling.

In a mixing bowl, beat the egg whites into snowy peaks using an electric hand mixer. When they start to stiffen, gradually add the superfine sugar and spice blend, beating constantly. Strain the almond-sugar mixture over the egg whites and fold in using a silicone spatula.

Fill a pastry bag with this mixture and pipe out 30 x 1½-inch (4.5-cm) uniform circles onto a baking sheet lined with baking parchment. Let stand for at least 1 hour in a dry place until a crust forms on the surface. Sprinkle the shells with the reserved pumpkin pie spice blend, then cook for 10–12 minutes. Let the shells cool, then pour a trickle of water between the parchment and the baking sheet and remove the shells using a small frosting spatula.

TO ASSEMBLE THE MACAROONS Spread the apple confiture over half the shells, then top them with the remaining shells. Chill for 1 hour before serving.

PINEAPPLE AND SZECHUAN PEPPER MACAROON

The Szechuan pepper infusion complements the pineapple brilliantly. Both sweet and spicy, this original macaroon will astonish your guests.

PREPARATION TIME 40 minutes
INFUSING TIME 20 minutes
CHILLING TIME 12–24 hours
    + 1 hour
SHELL DRYING TIME 1 hour
COOKING TIME about 25 minutes

FOR THE SHELLS

2 large eggs
½ cup (60 g) ground almonds
¾ cup (110 g) confectioners' sugar
1½ tablespoons (20 g)
    superfine sugar
Yellow food coloring

FOR THE PEPPER GANACHE

3½ fl oz (100 ml) pineapple juice
1 teaspoon lime juice
2 teaspoons Szechuan peppercorns
2 eggs, yolks only
⅓ cup (150 g) superfine sugar
2 heaping teaspoons cornstarch

MAKES 15 MACAROONS

PREPARE AHEAD Separate the eggs and set the whites aside in the refrigerator for up to 24 hours. Bring to room temperature before making the macaroon shells the following day. Reserve the yolks to use in the ganache.

TO MAKE THE PEPPER GANACHE Put the pineapple and lime juice in a saucepan and bring to a boil, then add the peppercorns. Remove from the heat and let the mixture infuse for 20 minutes, then pass it through a fine-mesh conical sieve and set aside. In a mixing bowl, beat the egg yolks with the superfine sugar, add the cornstarch and the pineapple-lime juice, and blend in well. Pour the mixture into a saucepan and cook over a low heat for 5–7 minutes. Remove from the heat and let cool. Chill in the refrigerator.

TO MAKE THE SHELLS Preheat the oven to 300°F (150°C). Finely grind the ground almonds and confectioners' sugar in a blender. Strain the mixture over a baking sheet and cook for 5–7 minutes. Let cool.

In a mixing bowl, beat the egg whites into snowy peaks using an electric hand mixer. When they start to stiffen, gradually add the superfine sugar, beating constantly. Add a few drops of yellow food coloring and combine until evenly dispersed. Strain the almond-sugar mixture over the egg whites and fold in using a silicone spatula.

Fill a pastry bag with this mixture and pipe out 30 x 1½-inch (4.5-cm) uniform circles onto a baking sheet lined with baking parchment. Let stand for at least 1 hour in a dry place until a crust forms on the surface, then cook for 10–12 minutes. Let the shells cool, then pour a trickle of water between the parchment and the baking sheet and remove the shells using a small frosting spatula.

TO ASSEMBLE THE MACAROONS Spread the ganache over half the shells, then top them with the remaining shells. Chill for 1 hour before serving.

COCONUT AND LIME MACAROON

Unlike other recipes, this one does not use any food coloring. What's more, the macaroons are cooked at a lower temperature than usual; this way they will retain their pretty pale color.

PREPARATION TIME 30 minutes
CHILLING TIME 12–24 hours
  + 1 hour
SHELL DRYING TIME 1 hour
COOKING TIME about 30 minutes

FOR THE SHELLS

2 large eggs
⅓ cup (40 g) ground almonds
¾ cup (110 g) confectioners' sugar
2 tablespoons (40 g) shredded
  dried coconut
1½ tablespoons (20 g)
  superfine sugar

FOR THE LIME GANACHE

4 heaping tablespoons (60 g)
  turbinado sugar
2 eggs
1 heaping tablespoon cornstarch
Juice of 4 limes

MAKES 15 MACAROONS

PREPARE AHEAD Separate the eggs and set the whites aside in the refrigerator for up to 24 hours. Bring to room temperature before making the macaroon shells the following day.

TO MAKE THE LIME GANACHE In a mixing bowl, beat together the turbinado sugar and the eggs. Add the cornstarch and the lime juice, then pour into a saucepan. Cook for 5–10 minutes over a low heat, stirring constantly. Remove from the heat and refrigerate when cool.

TO MAKE THE SHELLS Preheat the oven to 300°F (150°C). Finely grind the ground almonds, confectioners' sugar, and half the shredded coconut in a blender. Strain the mixture over a baking sheet and cook for 5–7 minutes. Let cool.

Lower the oven temperature to 250°F (120°C). In a mixing bowl, beat the egg whites into snowy peaks using an electric hand mixer. When they start to stiffen, gradually add the superfine sugar, beating constantly. Strain the almond-sugar-coconut blend over the egg whites and fold in using a silicone spatula.

Fill a pastry bag with this mixture and pipe out 30 x 1½-inch (4.5-cm) uniform circles onto a baking sheet lined with baking parchment. Let stand for at least 1 hour in a dry place until a crust forms on the surface. Sprinkle the shells with the reserved shredded coconut, then cook for 12–15 minutes. Let the shells cool, then pour a trickle of water between the parchment and the baking sheet and remove the shells using a small frosting spatula.

TO ASSEMBLE THE MACAROONS Spread the lime ganache over half the shells, then top them with the remaining shells. Chill for 1 hour before serving.

KIWI AND BANANA MACAROON

A successful combination of sweet and sharp flavors, this fruity macaroon is a guilt-free feast.

PREPARATION TIME 30 minutes
CHILLING TIME 12–24 hours
    + 1 hour
SHELL DRYING TIME 1 hour
COOKING TIME about 30 minutes

FOR THE SHELLS

2 large eggs
½ cup (60 g) ground almonds
¾ cup (110 g) confectioners' sugar
1½ tablespoons (20 g)
    superfine sugar
Green food coloring

FOR THE KIWI FRUIT GANACHE

2 small kiwi fruit, peeled and diced
½ banana, peeled and sliced
Scant ½ cup (100 g) superfine sugar
2 tablespoons (30 g) pectin or other
    gelling agent for jams

MAKES 15 MACAROONS

PREPARE AHEAD Separate the eggs and set the whites aside in the refrigerator for up to 24 hours. Bring to room temperature before making the macaroon shells the following day.

TO MAKE THE KIWI FRUIT GANACHE Put the kiwi fruit, banana, and half the superfine sugar in a saucepan and cook gently until soft. Let cool slightly, then blend with a hand blender. Return to the saucepan, add the remaining superfine sugar and the pectin, and cook for 5 minutes over a low heat. Remove from the heat and refrigerate when cool.

TO MAKE THE SHELLS Preheat the oven to 300°F (150°C). Finely grind the ground almonds and confectioners' sugar in a blender. Strain the mixture over a baking sheet and cook for 5–7 minutes. Let cool.

In a mixing bowl, beat the egg whites into snowy peaks, using an electric hand mixer. When they start to stiffen, gradually add the superfine sugar, beating constantly. Add a few drops of green food coloring and combine until evenly dispersed. Strain the almond-sugar mixture over the egg whites and fold in using a silicone spatula.

Fill a pastry bag with this mixture and pipe out 30 x 1½-inch (4.5-cm) uniform circles onto a baking sheet lined with baking parchment. Let stand for at least 1 hour in a dry place until a crust forms on the surface, then cook for 10–12 minutes. Let the shells cool, then pour a trickle of water between the parchment and the baking sheet and remove the shells using a small frosting spatula.

TO ASSEMBLE THE MACAROONS Spread the kiwi fruit ganache over half the shells, then top them with the remaining shells. Chill for 1 hour before serving.

ORANGE AND GINGER MACAROON

For added zing, either sprinkle the shells with powdered ginger before cooking, or add a teaspoon of this deliciously warming spice to the shell mixture.

PREPARATION TIME 30 minutes
CHILLING TIME 12–24 hours
    + 1 hour
SHELL DRYING TIME 1 hour
COOKING TIME about 25 minutes

FOR THE SHELLS

2 large eggs
½ cup (60 g) ground almonds
¾ cup (110 g) confectioners' sugar
1½ tablespoons (20 g)
    superfine sugar
Orange food coloring

FOR THE ORANGE GANACHE

2 eggs
4 scant tablespoons (50 g)
    turbinado sugar
1 heaping teaspoon cornstarch
1 teaspoon powdered ginger
Juice of 2 oranges
1½ tablespoons (20 g) butter,
    diced small

MAKES 15 MACAROONS

PREPARE AHEAD Separate the eggs and set the whites aside in the refrigerator for up to 24 hours. Bring to room temperature before making the macaroon shells the following day.

TO MAKE THE ORANGE GANACHE In a mixing bowl, beat the eggs and turbinado sugar together. Add the cornstarch, ginger, and orange juice. Pour into a saucepan and cook over a low heat for 5–7 minutes, stirring constantly. When the mixture thickens, add the butter and beat in well. Remove from the heat and let cool. Chill in the refrigerator.

TO MAKE THE SHELLS Preheat the oven to 300°F (150°C). Finely grind the ground almonds and confectioners' sugar in a blender. Strain the mixture over an oven tray and cook for 5–7 minutes. Let cool.

In a mixing bowl, beat the egg whites into snowy peaks using an electric hand mixer. When they start to stiffen, gradually add the superfine sugar, beating constantly. Add a few drops of orange food coloring and combine until evenly dispersed. Strain the almond-sugar mixture over the egg whites and fold in using a silicone spatula.

Fill a pastry bag with this mixture and pipe out 30 x 1½-inch (4.5-cm) uniform circles onto a baking sheet lined with baking parchment. Let stand for at least 1 hour in a dry place until a crust forms on the surface, then cook for 10–12 minutes. Let the shells cool, then pour a trickle of water between the parchment and the baking sheet and remove the shells using a small frosting spatula.

TO ASSEMBLE THE MACAROONS Spread the orange ganache over half the shells, then top them with the remaining shells. Chill for 1 hour before serving.

FIG AND ORANGE FLOWER MACAROON

Here's a sunny recipe to serve at summer tea-parties.
Serve these macaroons accompanied by fresh homemade
lemonade or an orange flower tea.

PREPARATION TIME 30 minutes
CHILLING TIME 12–24 hours
    + 1 hour
SHELL DRYING TIME 1 hour
COOKING TIME about 35 minutes

FOR THE SHELLS

2 large eggs
½ cup (60 g) ground almonds
¾ cup (110 g) confectioners' sugar
1½ tablespoons (20 g)
    superfine sugar
1 teaspoon orange flower water

FOR THE FIG CONFITURE

5 figs, washed and chopped
2 tablespoons orange flower water
4 scant tablespoons (50 g)
    superfine sugar
2 teaspoons (10 g) pectin or other
    gelling agent for jams

MAKES 15 MACAROONS

PREPARE AHEAD Separate the eggs and set the whites aside in the refrigerator for up to 24 hours. Bring to room temperature before making the macaroon shells the following day.

TO MAKE THE FIG CONFITURE Put the figs in a saucepan with the orange flower water, superfine sugar, and 1 tablespoon of water. Cook for 10–12 minutes over a low heat, let cool slightly, then blend to a purée. Return to the saucepan, add the pectin, and cook for 2–3 minutes more. Remove from the heat and refrigerate when cool.

TO MAKE THE SHELLS Preheat the oven to 300°F (150°C). Finely grind the ground almonds and confectioners' sugar in a blender. Strain the mixture over a baking sheet and cook for 5–7 minutes. Let cool.
  In a mixing bowl, beat the egg whites into snowy peaks using an electric hand mixer. When they start to stiffen, gradually add the superfine sugar, beating constantly. Add the orange flower water and blend in well. Strain the almond-sugar mixture over the egg whites and fold in using a silicone spatula.
  Fill a pastry bag with this mixture and pipe out 30 x 1½-inch (4.5-cm) uniform circles onto a baking sheet lined with baking parchment. Let stand for at least 1 hour in a dry place until a crust forms on the surface, then cook for 10–12 minutes. Let the shells cool, then pour a trickle of water between the parchment and the baking sheet and remove the shells using a small frosting spatula.

TO ASSEMBLE THE MACAROONS Spread the fig confiture over half the shells, then top them with the remaining shells. Chill for 1 hour before serving.

ALMOND AND MAPLE SYRUP MACAROON

This sweet and sugary macaroon has subtle undertones. If desired, the maple syrup in the ganache can be replaced with honey, preferably a flowery one.

PREPARATION TIME 30 minutes
CHILLING TIME 12–24 hours
   + 3 hours + 1 hour
SHELL DRYING TIME 1 hour
COOKING TIME about 20 minutes

FOR THE SHELLS

2 large eggs
½ cup (60 g) ground almonds
¾ cup (110 g) confectioners' sugar
1½ tablespoons (20 g)
   superfine sugar
Brown food coloring

FOR THE MAPLE SYRUP GANACHE

2 leaves gelatin
Scant ½ cup (100 ml) maple syrup
2 eggs, yolks only
3 teaspoons (15 g) superfine sugar
1 cup (250 ml) whipping
   cream, chilled

MAKES 15 MACAROONS

PREPARE AHEAD Separate the eggs and set the whites aside in the refrigerator for up to 24 hours. Bring to room temperature before making the macaroon shells the following day. Reserve the yolks to use in the ganache.

TO MAKE THE MAPLE SYRUP GANACHE Steep the gelatin in a bowl of cold water. In a saucepan, heat the maple syrup gently over a low heat, then remove from the heat and add the drained gelatin. Whisk the egg yolks with 1 teaspoon of superfine sugar and add them to the warm maple syrup-gelatin mix. Beat the whipping cream and the remaining sugar until firm, then pour into the maple syrup mixture and blend in well. Let cool, then chill in the refrigerator for at least 3 hours.

TO MAKE THE SHELLS Preheat the oven to 300°F (150°C). Finely grind the ground almonds and confectioners' sugar in a blender. Strain the mixture over a baking sheet and cook for 5–7 minutes. Let cool.
   In a mixing bowl, beat the egg whites into snowy peaks using an electric hand mixer. When they start to stiffen, gradually add the superfine sugar, beating constantly. Add a few drops of brown food coloring and combine until evenly dispersed. Strain the almond-sugar mixture over the egg whites and fold in using a silicone spatula.
   Fill a pastry bag with this mixture and pipe out 30 x 1½-inch (4.5-cm) uniform circles onto a baking sheet lined with baking parchment. Let stand for at least 1 hour in a dry place until a crust forms on the surface, then cook for 10–12 minutes. Let the shells cool, then pour a trickle of water between the parchment and the baking sheet and remove the shells using a small frosting spatula.

TO ASSEMBLE THE MACAROONS Spread the maple syrup ganache over half the shells, then top them with the remaining shells. Chill for 1 hour before serving.

CARROT AND WALNUT MACAROON

Make your own carrot juice by puréeing carrots, preferably organic, with a little water and a large squeeze of lemon juice to stop the juice going brown. Strain off the juice.

PREPARATION TIME 30 minutes
CHILLING TIME 12–24 hours
  + 1 hour + 1 hour
SHELL DRYING TIME 1 hour
COOKING TIME about 20 minutes

FOR THE SHELLS

2 large eggs
½ cup (60 g) ground almonds
¾ cup (110 g) confectioners' sugar
1½ tablespoons (20 g)
  superfine sugar
Copper food coloring

FOR THE CARROT GANACHE

7 oz (200 g) white chocolate
1 tablespoon whipping cream
3 generous tablespoons (50 ml)
  organic carrot juice
Juice of ½ lemon
2 tablespoons (20 g) chopped
  walnuts

MAKES 15 MACAROONS

PREPARE AHEAD Separate the eggs and set the whites aside in the refrigerator for up to 24 hours. Bring to room temperature before making the macaroon shells the following day.

TO MAKE THE CARROT GANACHE Break the chocolate into small pieces, and melt gently with the whipping cream in a bowl set over a pan of barely simmering water. Add the carrot and lemon juice and blend in well, then add the chopped walnuts. Remove from the heat and refrigerate when cool.

TO MAKE THE SHELLS Preheat the oven to 300°F (150°C). Finely grind the ground almonds and confectioners' sugar in a blender. Strain the mixture over a baking sheet and cook for 5–7 minutes. Let cool.

In a mixing bowl, beat the egg whites into snowy peaks using an electric hand mixer. When they start to stiffen, gradually add the superfine sugar, beating constantly. Add a few drops of copper food coloring and combine until evenly dispersed. Strain the almond-sugar mixture over the egg whites and fold in using a silicone spatula.

Fill a pastry bag with this mixture and pipe out 30 x 1½-inch (4.5-cm) uniform circles onto a baking sheet lined with baking parchment. Let stand for at least 1 hour in a dry place until a crust forms on the surface, then cook for 10–12 minutes. Let the shells cool, then pour a trickle of water between the parchment and the baking sheet and remove the shells using a small frosting spatula.

TO ASSEMBLE THE MACAROONS Spread the carrot ganache over half the shells, then top them with the remaining shells. Chill for 1 hour before serving.

An Hachette UK Company
First published in Great Britain in 2010 by Spruce
a division of Octopus Publishing Group Ltd
Endeavour House, 189 Shaftesbury Avenue, London, WC2H 8JY
www.octopusbooks.co.uk

Distributed in the U.S.A. and Canada for Octopus Books USA
c/- Hachette Book Group USA
237 Park Avenue
New York, NY 10017

This material was first published as *Macarons* by Albums Larousse 2009

Design © Octopus Publishing Group Ltd 2010
Text and photography copyright © Larousse 2010

CONSULTANT PUBLISHER Sarah Ford
MANAGING EDITOR Camilla Davis
TRANSLATED BY JMS Book llp
    TRANSLATOR Sheila Murphy
    EDITOR Jenni Davis
DESIGNER Simon Daley
PHOTOGRAPHER Marie-José Jarry
PRODUCTION Caroline Alberti

ISBN 13 978-1-84601-383-6
ISBN 10 1-84601-383-6

A CIP catalogue record for this book is available from the British Library.

Printed and bound in China

10 9 8 7 6 5 4 3 2 1

This book includes macaroons made with nuts. It is advisable for those
with known allergic reactions to nuts and those who may be potentially
vulnerable to these allergies, such as pregnant and nursing mothers, the
elderly, babies, and children, to avoid these items.